Bats

Published by Wildlife Education, Ltd.
12233 Thatcher Court, Poway, California 92064
contact us at: **1-800-477-5034**
e-mail us at: **animals@zoobooks.com**
visit us at: **www.zoobooks.com**

ISBN 1-888153-48-2

Bats

Series Created by
John Bonnett Wexo

Written by
Linda C. Wood
Deane Rink

Scientific Consultant
Merlin D. Tuttle, Ph.D.
Bat Conservation International
P.O. Box 162603
Austin, Texas 78716

Contents

Bats are a mystery to most people. In fact, many people have never even *seen* a bat up close. Yet there are bats living all over the United States—and in most other countries of the world. Why do people know so little about bats?

The biggest reason is that bats are *nocturnal*—they sleep in the daytime and hunt at night. And they are shy. It's hard to find them, and even harder to study them. So scientists still don't know much about them.

But we do know that bats are about the most misunderstood animals in the world. Many people don't like them. And some people are terrified of them—probably because they have seen pictures of bats with scary-looking faces.

But as strange as bats sometimes look, they are not frightening or dangerous animals. In fact, they are actually very gentle. And they do a lot of good for people.

For one thing, bats are the world's most important predators of night-flying insects. They eat mosquitoes and many of the bugs that destroy our crops. If it weren't for bats, there would be far too many insects in the world.

For another thing, fruit-and-nectar-eating bats scatter the seeds of some of our favorite fruits. And they pollinate many beautiful trees and tropical shrubs. If it weren't for bats, tropical forests would not be as lush and green. And we might not have bananas, figs, avocados, cashew nuts, and many other wonderful foods.

But that's not all there is to admire about bats. They are also the only *mammals* that can fly! For this reason, many people think that they are birds. But bats actually belong to the same animal group, or *class*, as dogs, cats, and humans. This class is known as Mammalia.

Like all mammals, bats are warm-blooded. They have fur to help keep them warm in cold weather. And their babies are born alive (instead of being hatched from eggs).

As you can see, bats are both fascinating and valuable animals. And this book will tell you about what makes them such wonderful and mysterious creatures.

MEXICAN FREE-TAILED BATS

Bats have always played an important part in human myths. Because bats are nocturnal animals, people have even thought of them as evil spirits—friends of witches, vampires, ghosts, and other creatures of the night.

Today we know that bats are not evil spirits. Yet so many unkind things have been said about bats over the years that many people still have the wrong idea about them. Through the ages, the stories have been greatly exaggerated. It's important to know the truth about these interesting animals.

Bats were once thought to have evil powers. So many fairy tales and legends tell how witches used bat wings to make their evil brews. But bats are not evil animals. They're really no different from any other kind of animal.

Have you ever heard the saying "as blind as a bat"? Well, don't believe it. Bats can see quite well—even on the darkest of nights. Some see with their eyes, and some "see" with their ears.

Another tall tale about bats is that they often get tangled up in people's hair. But this is silly. Bats have no interest at all in getting in your hair.

Some people think that bats are flying rodents. But they're wrong. Bats are so different from anything else that scientists have put them in an *order* (Chiroptera) all by themselves. Even humans don't have an order of their own.

In stories and movies, bats always surround the vampire Dracula. At times, he even changes into a bat himself. But everyone knows that vampires are not real. And even vampire bats rarely feed on human blood.

Many people think that bats are dirty animals. But just the opposite is true. Bats are actually incredibly clean animals that spend a lot of time grooming themselves.

You might have heard that all bats carry rabies. This is not true. Bats can get rabies, but no more easily than any other wild animal. Still, you should *never touch a bat you find on the ground*. It could be sick, and might try to bite you if it is frightened.

There are nearly a thousand different kinds, or *species*, of bats in the world. Almost one in every four mammal species is a bat! A few of the more common species are shown on these pages.

Bats come in an amazing variety of shapes and sizes. And they are found in more climates and habitats than almost any other animal. Most bats live in warm tropical areas, where there are many insects, fruits, and flowers. But bats are also found in swamps, deserts, grasslands, and even in very cold regions of the world.

Some common bat "homes" are caves, tall trees, bushes, barns, and fence posts. A few bats live in very unusual places, like hollow termite nests or spider webs. And some even make their own homes by cutting leaves to make "tents."

Bats are found on every continent of the world except Antarctica. About 40 species of bats live in the United States and Canada.

PALLID BAT
Antrozous pallidus
(WESTERN UNITED STATES AND MEXICO)

COMMON FLYING FOX
Pteropus vampyrus
(JAVA)

KITTI'S HOG-NOSED BAT
Craseonycteris thonglongyai
(THAILAND)

SMALLEST

LARGEST

The largest bat in the world weighs about two pounds and has a wingspan of six feet! The smallest bat is the size of a bumblebee and weighs less than a penny! Both of these bats live in Asia.

JAMAICAN FRUIT BAT
Artibeus jamaicensis
(MEXICO, CENTRAL AMERICA, AND SOUTH AMERICA)

FISHING BULLDOG BAT
Noctilio leporinus
(MEXICO, CENTRAL AMERICA,
AND SOUTH AMERICA)

MEXICAN FREE-TAILED BAT
Tadarida brasiliensis
(SOUTHERN UNITED STATES,
MEXICO, AND CENTRAL AMERICA)

TENT-BUILDING BAT
Uroderma bilobatum
(CENTRAL AND SOUTH AMERICA)

DOBSON'S HORSESHOE BAT
Rhinolophus yumanensis
(ASIA)

SHEATH-TAILED BAT
Balantiopteryx plicata
(MEXICO AND CENTRAL AMERICA)

DAWN BAT
Eonycteris spelaea
(SOUTHEAST ASIA)

LESSER LONG-NOSED BAT
Leptonycteris curasoae
(SOUTHWESTERN UNITED STATES
AND MEXICO)

11

FLYING SQUIRREL

Flying squirrels can jump out of trees and *glide* through the air. But they can't really fly. Instead of having true wings like bats do, they just have flaps of skin that stretch from their arms to their legs.

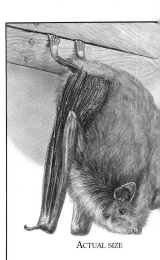

ACTUAL SIZE

BAT ANCESTORS

The ancestors of bats were probably primitive *insectivores* that lived in trees and ate insects. But bats are very ancient, because the earliest known bat lived about *50 million years ago*, and it was only slightly different than the bats of today.

The body of a bat is perfectly suited for flying. Like birds, bats have lightweight bones and small bodies, so they have less weight to carry when they fly. And they have *true wings* to help them fly. But unlike bird wings, which are made of feathers, bat wings are *made of skin*! When fully stretched out, a bat's wings can be three to four times the length of its body! And a bat's wings, nose, and ears are the only parts of its body not covered with fur.

Some bats take off from the ground, but most launch themselves from a tree, cave, or barn roof.

When flying, bats can reach altitudes of *10,000 feet*. And if the winds are right, they can go as fast as *60 miles per hour*!

Bats use their wings to pull themselves through the air, the way swimmers use their arms to pull themselves through the water. If you have ever used the butterfly stroke, then you know how a flying bat moves its wings.

Like the swimming muscles of a swimmer, the main flight muscles of a bat are located in the chest and back.

12

Most bats are small enough to fit in your hand—they weigh only an ounce or less. The head of this *Myotis* bat is no bigger than a dime! Like other bats, *Myotis* bats sleep by hanging from their feet.

Bats use their claw-like thumbs to help them move across rough surfaces like cave walls and tree bark.

All bats have special tendons in their legs that make it possible for them to hang upside down, or *roost*. This enables them to live in places like cave ceilings, where dangerous predators cannot get to them.

THUMB

Bats have long, curved claws on their feet. They use these for roosting, climbing, and grooming.

Bat wings are so thin that you can almost see through them. But don't let this fool you. A bat's wing is actually tougher than a rubber glove. If bat wings weren't so tough, sharp objects like thorns and twigs could easily tear them.

Bats fly with their hands!
The bones in a bat's wing are like the bones in your arm and hand—except that bats have incredibly long fingers. Two thin layers of skin stretched out between these fingers form a bat's wing.

13

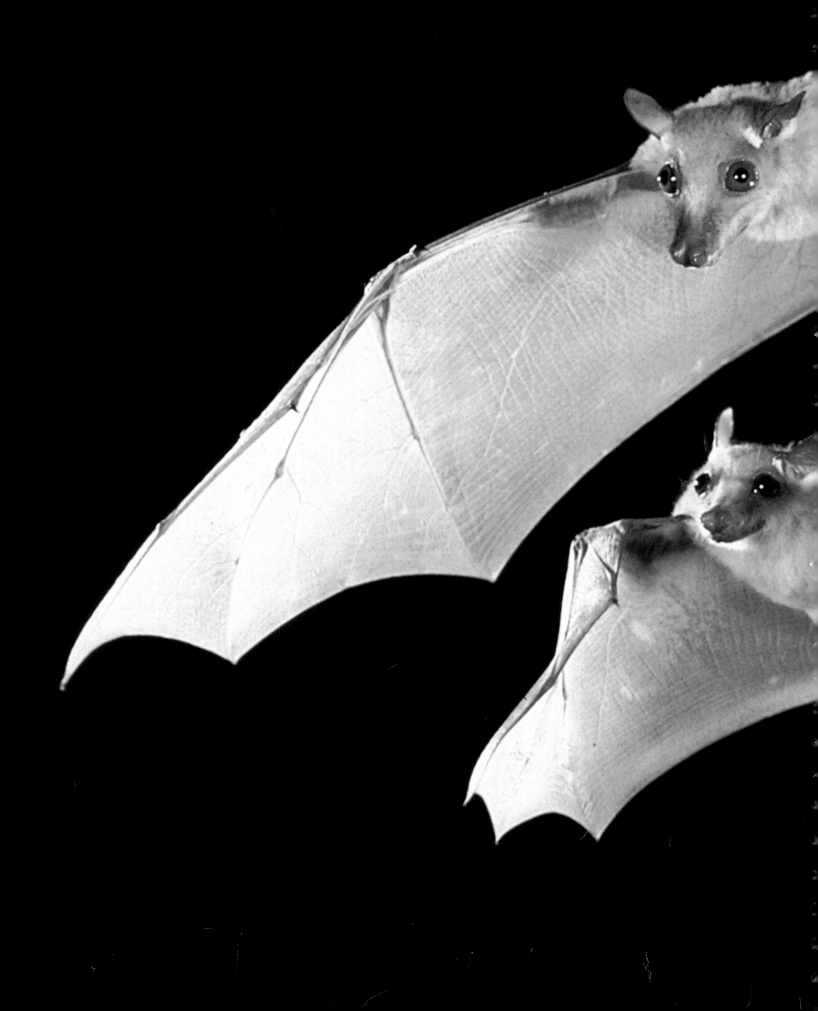

A mother bat and her baby. These bats are called "flying foxes" because of their fox-like faces.

*I*f bats hunt at night, then what do they do in the daytime? Most bats sleep during the warmer daylight hours, saving their energy until the evening. About half of all bats in the United States live in caves. Caves make good roosting places, because they are dark and usually quiet. But trees and buildings can be good roosting places, too.

Many bats go into a deep sleep, or *hibernate*, during the cold winter months. They have enough energy stored in their body fat to last them until spring. But if they are disturbed while hibernating, they will lose precious amounts of this energy. And if they lose too much of it, they could die.

Many bats form nursery colonies to care for their young. When the mothers go out to hunt, the babies cluster together to stay warm.

Sometimes, *millions* of bats live together in a cave. When roosting, their bodies are packed together like sardines. There may be as many as *300 bats per square foot!*

For the first few weeks of their lives, baby bats live on their mother's milk. Mother bats, like all mammals, produce their milk in special glands called *mammary glands*.

Most bats carry their babies only when

Some bats feel right at home in human structures—like barns, attics, and buildings. The bats above have found a cozy "hang out" on the underside of a roof.

In warm tropical countries, fruit-eating bats like these can often be seen hanging from tree branches.

Come on, let's just go in and take a peek.

No! How would you like it if somebody woke you up when you were sleeping?

STAY OUT
BATS SLEEPING

Many people do not realize that visiting a cave where bats are hibernating or raising their young can be very harmful to the bats inside. *Thousands of bats die each year because people wake them. Never disturb roosting bats!*

People can help bats by building bat houses that give them additional places to roost. For more information about bats and bat houses, write to: Bat Conservation International, P. O. Box 162603, Austin, TX 78716.

17

For years, people wondered how bats could fly at night without crashing into things. Did they have some special kind of night vision to help them? In the 1930s, scientists discovered that bats have a kind of natural sonar that allows them to "see" with their ears! Using only sound, bats can follow and catch prey *in total darkness*! This amazing sonar system is called *echolocation*.

Not all bats have the ability for echolocation. For instance, most fruit-eating bats rely on sight and smell to get around and find food. They don't need echolocation because they don't hunt moving prey.

1

When hunting for insects, a bat sends out a series of squeaking sounds, or *ultrasonic pulses*, through its mouth or nose. Most of these pulses are so high-pitched that a human being can't hear them. Jet fighter planes use a similar technique to detect enemy missiles.

Most bats send out their signals through their mouths. But others use their noses. Many bats have funny-looking skin flaps on their faces that help to direct sound pulses.

3 A bat knows when an insect is near, because the sounds *echo*, or bounce, off of it and return to the bat's ears. When the bat hears the echo, it can tell exactly where the insect is located. In a similar way, a jet plane can tell exactly where an enemy missile is located.

2 "Scanning" for insects, the bat continues to send out pulses of sound—sometimes as many as *500 per second*!

A bat's echolocation system is so precise that it can detect an insect that is smaller than a mosquito. Some bats can detect objects that are *no wider than a human hair*!

Once the bat has zeroed in on its target, it goes in for the kill. It grabs the insect with its mouth, or scoops it up with its wings or tail membrane. Some insect-eating bats can catch as many as *3,000 insects in a single night*!

4

Special grooves inside the bat's ears help to channel the sounds that bounce off of the insect.

19

Bats love to eat—and they usually have huge appetites for their size. Like birds, bats *need* to eat a lot because they use up so much energy when they fly. Most bats are insect eaters. Their favorite foods are beetles, moths, flies, and mosquitoes—some even eat grasshoppers, crickets, and scorpions! Other bats, mostly those that live in tropical forests, eat fruit or drink the nectar from flowers. A few bats are meat eaters. They dine on fish, frogs, mice, and birds. And a very small number of bats feed on the blood of large animals—these bats are found only in Latin America.

All bats need water as well as food. Many bats drink water by flying low over a stream or lake and dipping their mouths into the surface. Others get water from the fruits or insects they eat.

Vampire bats, like the one at left, feed on sleeping animals— usually cows or horses. The bat spots an animal and lands near it. Then it "walks" up to it, makes a small cut in the animal's skin, and laps up some blood. The animal barely feels the "bite," and almost never wakes up.

Like insect-eating bats, fishing bats use echolocation to find their meals. First, the bat skims the surface of the water, sending out signals to detect small ripples where fish are feeding.

1

Bats that catch large insects often take them to a perch where they clip off the head, legs, and hard wing covers before eating the soft, tasty body. In just one night, a single bat can eat up to *half its body weight* in insects!

When it has located a fish, the bat swoops down low and drops its huge feet into the water, stabbing the prey with its sharp claws.

2

Some bats like to stuff themselves with fruit. In just one night, these epaulet bats of Africa can eat *2½ times their weight in fruit!*

As they fly between feeding sites, fruit bats often drop seeds from the fruit to the ground below. Later, the seeds may sprout and grow into new trees. This helps to keep the forests thick and lush.

4

Fishing bats usually eat their meals as they fly. But sometimes they carry their catch to a perch before eating it.

3 Then the bat uses its feet to scoop up the fish and bring the prey to its mouth.

Nectar-eating bats have long tongues so that they can reach deep into flowers to get at the nectar. The bat above has a tongue that is almost as long as its body! While eating, nectar bats spread pollen from one flower to another. This helps the flowers to produce new seeds, which then grow into new plants.

Bats—good omens or symbols of evil? In Europe in the Middle Ages, people feared bats and thought they were evil. But to the civilizations of ancient Persia and China, bats meant good luck, long life, and happiness.

Whether or not you believe in the legends of good or evil, bats are good for the environment and for people. Bats pollinate plants, provide guano for fertilizer, and eat insect pests that destroy crops. But all over the world, bat populations are shrinking.

Bats are now extinct on some of their island homes and are threatened with extinction on others. Where there were once thousands of bats, there are now a few hundred. Several bat species in the United States are endangered. The decline in bat populations affects the well-being of human populations. To have fewer bats means that fewer plants are pollinated and fewer seeds are spread for renewed plant growth.

In many tropical countries, people have long eaten fruit bats for protein. There were always thousands of bats, and the few that were caught for food didn't harm the bat population. But hunting methods have changed. Today, hunters have guns and hunt bats not just for themselves, but also to sell or trade. Bats that are cave dwellers fare no better. They are easily trapped at the narrow entrances to their caves.

In Malaysia, fruit production has slowed because the pollinating bats are being caught in large numbers with fishing nets stretched across their cave entrances. Besides the increase in hunting, bat habitats are being destroyed. This means the bats have fewer food sources, and their roosting trees are being cut down. Their caves are also at risk from limestone quarrying. In some countries, the sale of bat guano as fertilizer provides income to local people. With fewer bats, there is less guano to sell.

Some attempts are underway to stop the decline. A breeding colony has been established for at least one endangered bat, and bats are now protected throughout Europe and in many other countries. An organization called Bat Conservation International works to counter the myths about bats being evil and points out the good that comes from bats. This organization's research and education programs encourage people to help bats instead of harming them. You can help by sharing the truth about bats with your friends.

CALIFORNIA LEAF-NOSED BAT

Index

Meade Heights
Media Center

Nancy Paulsen Books
an imprint of Penguin Random House LLC
375 Hudson Street
New York, NY 10014

Nancy Paulsen Books is a registered trademark of Penguin Random House LLC.

Library of Congress Cataloging-in-Publication Data is available upon request.

Manufactured in China by RR Donnelley Asia Printing Solutions Ltd.
ISBN 9781101996683
10 9 8 7 6 5 4 3

Design by Jaclyn Reyes.
Text set in Atelier Sans ITC Std.
The illustrations were done in oil and collage, using tissue paper
and patterned papers created with homemade stamps.

For Bobbi Gibb, the girl who ran
—A.B.P.

Dedicated to Chella
—M.A.

Bobbi Gibb must wear a skirt to school because she is a girl. She is not allowed to run on the school's track team. Because those are the rules—and rules are rules.

But after school . . .

. . . Bobbi leaves the rules behind. She changes into pants and runs in the woods. Her feet crunch on frozen ground. She loves to twist through the trees like a bounding deer. The wind rushes past her ears.

She is fast.

HOPKINTON

ASHLAND   FRAMINGHAM   NATICK

WELLESLEY

Every spring, the Boston
Marathon winds through a
neighborhood not far from
Bobbi's house. One year
she goes to watch.
26.2 miles!
Can people
even run
that far?

HOPKINTON   ASHLAND   FRAMINGHAM   NATICK

WEL

MILES   1   2   3   4   5   6   7   8   9   10   11   12   1

Here come the runners! Bobbi's legs twitch to join the race.

SLEY   NEWTON   BROOKLINE   BOSTON

14 15 16 17 18 19 20 21 22 23 24 25 262

The day after the marathon, Bobbi starts to train.

She has no running shoes, no exercise clothes. But that doesn't stop Bobbi. She laces on sturdy nurses' shoes and starts to run.

She runs along city roads, covering longer distances every day.

People stare.

Is that a *girl* running?

Bobbi runs faster to escape the stares.

But mostly she runs because it makes her feel free.

FASHION

BEAUTY

Spring
SALE

In the summer, Bobbi takes a trip across the country. Each day,
she finds a place to run. She laces on her nurses' shoes and runs . . .
up and down rolling hills in Pennsylvania . . .
next to wide cornfields in Indiana . . .
along mountain trails in Colorado . . .
on the wet beach in California.

"I have run across an entire continent," she crows.

Winter back in Boston
brings bitter cold.

But it doesn't stop Bobbi. She swaps her nurses' shoes for boots and wears two pairs of mittens. She runs through snow and ice.

Now, fifteen or twenty miles is an easy day of running. Sometimes Bobbi runs thirty or even forty miles at a time.

She is ready for the Boston Marathon! She requests an application.

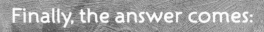
Finally, the answer comes:

We will not be able to send you an application. Women are not physiologically able to run twenty-six miles and furthermore the rules do not allow it.

Bobbi crumples the letter
and hurls it across the room.
She races out the door.

After hours of running,
Bobbi realizes something.
She has a chance to show the world
the rules are wrong.
She has a chance to show what women *can* do.
She *will* run the Boston Marathon.

For the race, Bobbi decides she needs real running shoes. Since they don't make them for girls, she buys a pair of size six boys' shoes. New shoes will make her feet feel weightless, she thinks.

She also finds a baggy sweatshirt that she hopes will help her blend in with the men.

Finally, it is race day!

Bobbi hides behind some bushes while the registered runners gather near the starting line.

Bang! The starting gun fires and Bobbi stumbles out of the bushes to join the race!

34

START

miles   1   2

elevation

400 ft.

300 ft.

200 ft.

100 ft.

0 ft.

Before long, Bobbi hears some of the runners whisper.

"Is that a girl?"

She smiles nervously at them.

They grin back. "It *is* a girl!"

"Great!"

They match her pace so they can run together.

"Are you going the whole way?"

"I hope so!"

The sweatshirt is too hot. But Bobbi is afraid to take it off.

What if officials see a girl is running?

201

400 ft. 3

300 ft.

200 ft.

100 ft.

0 ft.

4

5

6

The other runners reassure her. "Take it off."
"We won't let them throw you out."
Bobbi flings away the sweatshirt. Onlookers notice.
They cheer and scream for Bobbi. "It's a girl!"
"There's a girl running!"
"Go get 'em!"

16

7   8   9   10

Soon, everyone listening to the radio knows.
"A girl is running the Boston Marathon!"

11   12   13   14

400 ft.
300 ft.
200 ft.
100 ft.
0 ft.

The marathon route passes a women's college, Wellesley. The students are waiting for Bobbi.

"There she is!" They wave and shout.

"Do it, girl! Go! Go! Go! Go!"

15   16   17   18

Nineteen miles. Twenty miles. Up Heartbreak Hill. Bobbi feels confident. She is still running strong.

But coming downhill, things change.

Bobbi learns the hard way that you should not race in new shoes. Her feet are covered with blisters that pop and bleed.

Every step burns.

She can barely move for the pain, but she never considers stopping. She will finish this race if she has to crawl.

400 ft.
300 ft.
200 ft.
100 ft.
0 ft.

19   20   21   22

23   24   25   2 6.1

When Bobbi crosses the finish line on her bleeding feet, the crowd goes wild! The first woman has run the Boston Marathon!

It has taken her three hours and twenty minutes. She comes in 124th. Two hundred ninety-one men are still huffing and puffing their way to the finish line.

Cameras click.

Reporters scribble in their notebooks.

Even the governor of Massachusetts has come to the finish line to shake Bobbi's hand.

However, race officials refuse to give Bobbi a medal.
They insist that rules are rules.
But Bobbi has shown that it's time for some rules to change.
Bobbi has shown the world what women can do.
When they hear about Bobbi, other women and girls feel
their legs twitch. They want to join the race, too.

LIDIYA GRIGORYEVA

DIRE

LIANE WINTER

SARA MAE BERMAN

MIKI GOR

NINA KUSCSIK

UTA PIPPIG

FATUMA ROBA

SHARO

MARGARET OKAYO

TEYBA ERKESSO

RITA JEPTOO

WANDA PANFIL

S

Bobbi's first race is over,
but marathoning for
women has begun.

CAROLINE ROTICH

OLGA MARKOVA

ATSEDE BAYSA

UNE

KIM MERRITT

ROSA MOTA

INGRID KRISTIANSEN

N

JOAN BENOIT

CHEROP

LORRAINE MOLLER

CAROLINE KILEL

AYLE BARRON

SALINA KOSGEI

LISA RAINSBERGER

JACQUELINE HANSEN

EDNA KIPLAGAT

TLANA ZAKHAROVA

BOBBI GIBB